TIME FOR KIDS READERS

The Long Road to STATEHOOD!

House Sends
Bill to Ike

by Susan Kim

Harcourt

Orlando   Austin   Chicago   New York   Toronto   London   San Diego

Visit *The Learning Site!*
www.harcourtschool.com

"Land!"

It was January 18, 1778, and the sun had just begun to rise over the central Pacific Ocean. Many of the sailors aboard the British navy ship *Resolution* were waking up. Suddenly they heard a cry from atop one of the ship's three masts. "Land!" came the cry high above the deck. "Land!"

James Ward, the ship's lookout, had sighted the Hawaiian island of Oahu (oh•WAH•hoo). A few minutes later he spotted another Hawaiian island, Kauai (kah•WY). Ward was the first known European to set eyes on any of Hawaii's eight main islands. The first American to do so was John Gore, an officer aboard the *Resolution*.

This part of Kauai has probably changed very little since the island was first seen by the crew of the *Resolution*.

The *Resolution* had been sailing the Pacific for 18 months. Its captain was James Cook, one of the most successful explorers who ever lived. Hawaii was one of his greatest discoveries. Almost a year later, he returned and discovered a third island, Maui (MAU•ee). He named the islands the Sandwich Islands. Cook did this to honor a person who helped pay for his expedition—the Earl of Sandwich.

James Cook
1728–1779

What had Cook discovered? He couldn't have known it, but he had come across the longest chain of volcanic mountains in the world. Most of the mountains are far beneath the surface of the Pacific Ocean. All of them were made by molten rock that exploded through Earth's crust to form volcanoes. Those volcanic mountains form a chain 1,523 miles (2,451 km) long. The tops of some of those mountains poke through the water's surface.

Taller mountains have created eight large islands. The biggest of those islands, Hawaii—or Big Island—has more than 4,000 square miles (10,360 sq km) of surface. That makes it more than 3 times the size of the state of Rhode Island. Hawaii has two active volcanoes, Mauna Loa (MAW•nah LOH•uh) and Kilauea (key•lah•WAY•ah). They are both on Big Island. Mauna Kea, which is also on Big Island, is the world's tallest mountain if measured from the floor of the ocean to its peak. Honolulu, the capital of Hawaii, is located on Big Island.

The land area of the smallest main Hawaiian island, Kahoolawe (kah•hoh•ah•LAH•way), is 45 square miles (117 sq km). It is about the size of the city of San Francisco, California. The total land area of the other 6 islands is about 2,400 square miles (6,215 sq km). That makes them larger than the state of Delaware. Those 6 islands are Niihau (NEE•how), Kauai, Oahu, Maui, Molokai (moh•loh•KY), and Lanai (lu•NY). The only islands in the Hawaiian Islands chain that aren't part of Hawaii are the Midway Islands.

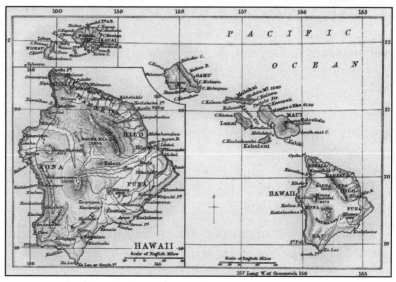

An early map shows the Hawaiian Islands.

Waikiki Beach in Honolulu, Hawaii, is always crowded with tourists.

Each island is unique. A huge volcano that became extinct about 6 million years ago created Kauai. More than a million years ago, Maui and Molokai were probably connected as a single huge island.

Niihau is privately owned. Only a few hundred people live on it. The earliest Hawaiians believed that Niihau was the home of the goddess Pele. Only one of the islands, Kahoolawe, is uninhabited. The United States Army and United States Navy used the island for target practice from 1941 until 1990. In 1993 the United States government began cleaning up the island and the waters around it. Hawaii took over the island in 1994.

More than 1.2 million people make their homes on the other six islands. The 8 islands, along with 124 smaller islands, make up the nation's fiftieth state, Hawaii.

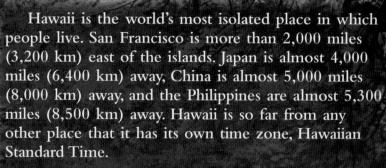

Hawaii is the world's most isolated place in which people live. San Francisco is more than 2,000 miles (3,200 km) east of the islands. Japan is almost 4,000 miles (6,400 km) away, China is almost 5,000 miles (8,000 km) away, and the Philippines are almost 5,300 miles (8,500 km) away. Hawaii is so far from any other place that it has its own time zone, Hawaiian Standard Time.

Being so cut off has made Hawaii far different from any other state. Its history is a story of brave Polynesian voyagers, kings, queens, foreign explorers, and fortune seekers. This rich history is set against a background of incredible beauty—volcanoes, ocean beaches, and tropical rain forests. It's no wonder that Hawaii is often called The Paradise of the Pacific.

Located in a rain forest on the island of Hawaii, Akaka Falls is 442 feet (135 m) high.

TFK
FAST FACTS
About Hawaii

Population More than 1.2 million

Capital Honolulu

Statehood August 21, 1959

Highest Point Mauna Kea, 13,796 feet (4,205 m)

Lowest Point Sea level

Nickname Aloha State

Motto The life of land is perpetuated in righteousness

Bird Hawaiian goose

Flower Yellow hibiscus

Tree Candlenut

The First Hawaiians

No one is sure when the first people went to Hawaii, or who they were. Some think they were from Polynesia, an area of widely scattered islands far to the south of Hawaii. Polynesians are thought to have sailed to Hawaii more than 1,500 years ago. Their name for the chain of islands was *Hawaii*. The name may have come from *owhyhee* (oh•WHY•ee), the Polynesians' word for *homeland*.

The early Hawaiians were skilled sailors, fishers, and farmers. They developed a clever way to irrigate, or water, their crops. They had their own language. Family, religion, and stories of their people's past were important to them. Today, experts still look closely at the songs passed from generation to generation to provide clues to how early Hawaiians lived and what they believed.

Early Hawaiians lived in houses made of grass, palm leaves, and wood.

Some Polynesians traveled to Hawaii in large sailboats.

For centuries, different kings ruled each Hawaiian island. Chiefs, or *alii* (AH•lee), were important, too, as were priests, or *kahuna* (KAH•oo•nah). Yet alii and kahuna were far less powerful than the kings. The kings sometimes sent warriors to fight people on other islands. They also went to war against strong alii on their own islands. The people of the islands enjoyed an uneasy peace for hundreds of years.

Captain Cook lost his life during a battle with Hawaiians in 1779. He was 51 years old.

The Discovery of Paradise

Hawaii's history was changed forever in 1778, when Captain James Cook happened to find the islands. Captain Cook claimed the islands for King George III, the British king. The British introduced new tools and ideas to the Hawaiians. Hawaiians quickly put metal tools such as saws, hammers, and plows to good use. By 1800 Hawaii was a stopping point for cargo ships sailing between the United States and China.

A young and ambitious king named Kamehameha (kah•MAY•hah•MAY•hah) used British guns to take over all the Hawaiian Islands. Kamehameha was the king of Big Island. In 1790 he managed to get hold of a schooner, a small ship with two masts. He mounted cannons on the schooner and armed his warriors with muskets, which enabled him to take control of the major islands one by one. By 1810 he was the sole king of

Hawaii. He is remembered today as the first person to bring all Hawaiians together under one government.

King Kamehameha was a wise ruler. During his rule, the islands prospered. Hawaiians earned money mainly from selling sandalwood to China. The Chinese prized sandalwood for its strong natural smell. Kamehameha also made money for his kingdom by charging merchants a tax for the goods they carried into Hawaii.

On the advice of the British, Kamehameha appointed governors to control the different islands for him. He also chose people to advise him on important issues.

Kamehameha welcomed many European ideas and goods. At the same time, he worried about losing the Hawaiian people's way of life. Protecting Hawaii's traditions became especially important after 1794. That's when Kamehameha and the alii agreed to let Britain protect the islands. As part of the agreement, Hawaiians kept the right to rule the islands on their own.

Hawaii's flag reflects the friendly relationship that developed between Hawaii and Britain. Created in 1816, the flag has eight stripes of white, red, and blue, representing the eight main islands. In the upper left corner is a miniature British flag. This is the official flag of the state of Hawaii today.

The state flag of Hawaii

King Kamehameha

Loosening the Ties to the Past

King Kamehameha died in 1819. Many people view his death as the beginning of the end of the old Hawaii. Now no one person or group had the ability to govern all of Hawaii. Outside forces were increasingly shaping life on the islands.

A missionary town sits in a bay in Honolulu, Hawaii.

One of those forces was Christianity. In 1820 a ship called *Thaddeus* arrived from Boston. It brought Christian missionaries, who were allowed by one of Kamehameha's successors to carry their message to Hawaiians. The missionaries brought mostly good changes to the region. They created the Hawaiian alphabet, which has only 12 letters: *a, e, i, o, u, h, k, l, m, n, p,* and *w.* They also set up schools and taught Hawaiians to read books, especially the Bible. [You may use some Hawaiian words such as *lei* (necklace of flowers), or *aloha* (hello), *hula* (dance), and *ukulele* (small guitar).]

During the next 80 years, Hawaiian monarchs did what they could to hold on to the traditional way, but gradually those traditions began to die out. The reason wasn't only the introduction of European ways. Diseases played a part, too. Europeans carried diseases such as measles, cholera, and typhus to Hawaii. Native Hawaiians had no resistance to them. During the century after Cook's arrival, diseases introduced by Europeans killed at least two-thirds of the native population.

TFK

Hawaiian Firts

- **1778** James Ward, a crew member on Captain James Cook's ship *Resolution*, is the first European known to see Hawaii.
- **1810** A play is staged in Hawaii.
- **1852** Steamship service carries passengers and goods between the islands.
- **1863** Elizabeth Sinclair, the first owner of Niihau, buys the island from King Kamehameha IV for $10,000.
- **1878** Telephone service begins.
- **1879** Freight train pulled by a locomotive carries sugar cane on Maui.
- **1886** Electric lights in Hawaii are strung around the Iolani Palace.
- **1901** Commercial pineapple plantation opens in central Oahu.
- **1901** Electric streetcars roll in Honolulu.
- **1910** An airplane flies for the first time in Hawaii.
- **1929** Airplane service between the islands begins.
- **1935** Airplane flies between San Francisco and Hawaii. Time in the air is almost 22 hours.

Europeans introduced sugar as a crop during the 1830s. Sugar production became a huge industry in Hawaii. It soon became more important to Hawaii's economy than fishing and other farm crops.

It was around this time that Hawaii's kings gave up their control of Hawaii's land. Before 1848 native Hawaiians and foreigners were allowed to lease land from the king. But no one, not even Hawaiian commoners, had the right to own land. In 1848 that system ended. Hawaiians were allowed to buy land. Foreigners were permitted to buy land in 1850. Because foreigners had the most money, they bought most of the best land. Without farmland of their own, native Hawaiians began to move to towns to find work.

Sugar was grown on huge plantations, which needed a great many workers. Because there weren't enough local workers, plantation owners began to import workers from China around 1852. Other immigrant groups arrived later. Among them were Japanese, Portuguese, Puerto Ricans, and Germans. Filipinos and Koreans went to Hawaii after 1900.

Immigrants worked on sugar cane plantations for small amounts of money.

As foreigners gained greater control of Hawaii's economy, they won more rights. But one thing they wanted more than any other was the power to run the government. They got that power in the early 1890s. At the time, Queen Liliuokalani (lih•lee•uh•woh•kuh•LAH•nee) was in charge. Queen Lili, as she was called, was a complicated person. A devout Christian, she was proud of her Hawaiian roots. She was also the talented composer of many beautiful songs.

Queen Lili was a brave leader. She tried to establish a body of laws that would return power to native Hawaiians. One problem was a deal that Hawaii had made with the United States in 1875. The United States had agreed not to tax Hawaiian sugar sold in the United States. Twelve years later, Hawaii gave the United States the right to use Pearl Harbor, on the island of Oahu.

Queen Lydia Liliuokalani

The arrangement was a boom to Hawaii's sugar industry. Yet the benefits granted to the sugar industry failed to satisfy foreign businesspeople. They knew they could make even more money if they controlled Hawaii's government. They forced Queen Liliuokalani out of power in 1893. The Kingdom of Hawaii, independent for 83 years, came to an end.

At the time, John Stevens represented the interests of the United States government in Hawaii. He became the head of Hawaii's new government. Stevens declared that Hawaii was formally under United States protection. Yet United States President Grover Cleveland was against making Hawaii part of the United States. Few Hawaiians supported the revolution, he said. Why should the United States?

Sanford Dole (1844–1926), shown here (third from left) with his Hawaiian Cabinet, was the president of Hawaii for four years.

In 1894 the temporary government refused to give up power. It made Sanford Dole president of Hawaii. A year later, supporters of Queen Lili made a bold attempt to restore her to the throne. The attempt was a failure, and Queen Lili was put under house arrest. She couldn't leave her palace for a full year. After the year was up, she lived as an ordinary citizen. She died in 1917.

Hawaiian Activities

1. Visit the U.S.S. *Arizona*, a memorial to the attack on Pearl Harbor.

2. See the royal possessions of Princess Bernice Pauahi Bishop, the last direct descendant of King Kamehameha.

3. Climb to the top of Diamond Head, an extinct volcano that was once a fort.

4. Snorkel in Hanauma Bay Nature Park, a sunken volcanic crater.

5. Check out a double-hull Polynesian voyaging canoe at the Hawaii Maritime Center.

6. Visit Iolani Palace, once Queen Liliuokalani's home and the only royal residence in the United States.

7. Take a whale-watching cruise.

8. Hold your breath while a daredevil dives off a 45-foot (14-m) waterfall at the Waimea Falls Park.

9. Learn to surf at a one-day surf school on a beautiful beach on the island of Maui.

10. Hike through a lava tube—a tunnel formed when the outside of a lava flow hardens and liquid lava continues to flow through it.

From Territory to State

Cleveland's successor, United States President William McKinley, liked the idea of annexing, or adding, Hawaii. In 1898 Hawaii came under United States control. The United States promised to make Hawaii a state someday. The first step, in 1900, was to make the islands a United States territory. Sanford Dole became the territory's first governor.

By this time, five big companies, the Big Five, controlled business on Hawaii. Sugar was still a huge business, but coffee growing and cattle ranching were important, too. Another growing business was canning pineapples for sale around the world. Today, more than 100 years later, those same businesses are still flourishing.

These young Hawaiian hula dancers became U.S. citizens at birth.

More than one-third of the world's pineapples come from Hawaii.

18

All these political changes made Hawaii a confusing place. Because Hawaii was a United States territory, men were allowed to vote in United States elections. Yet those men weren't United States citizens. All Hawaiians were still considered citizens of Hawaii.

Children born in the territory, however, became U.S. citizens at birth. So did the children of the workers who had come from China, Japan, and the Philippines. But their parents weren't Hawaiian citizens, nor were they citizens of the United States. They remained citizens of the countries they came from.

The Hawaiians born as United States citizens grew up and became a real political force in the territory. Many of them wanted Hawaii to become a state. In 1937 the United States Congress rejected the idea of statehood for Hawaii. Its members thought Hawaii was too far away to join the Union.

Everything changed for Hawaii on December 7, 1941. Japanese aircraft made a surprise attack on Pearl Harbor. More than 2,000 sailors and soldiers were killed as well as 68 civilians. Overnight, the United States found itself pulled into World War II. The Hawaiian Islands became the Pacific base for U.S. forces fighting in the Pacific.

After the attack on Pearl Harbor, the United States declared war on Japan.

World War II ended in 1945, and Hawaiians found that the war had made many changes. Farm and factory workers began to fight for more rights and better pay. They went on strike, walking away from their jobs, in 1946, 1949, and 1958. Even the dockworkers, who were needed to load ships with Hawaiian farm products, went on strike. With their businesses beginning to weaken, the owners met many of the workers' demands.

Improved air travel gave the tourist industry a big boost around this time. As fancy hotels and housing developments went up, the construction industry grew rapidly.

On January 3, 1959, Alaska became the forty-ninth state. Hawaii followed seven months later, becoming the fiftieth state on August 21, 1959. On Statehood Day, Hawaiians showed their pride in celebrations that swept through the islands. Small communities set bonfires, people danced in the streets, and car horns blared.

Today, Hawaii, like all 50 states, is constantly changing. Agriculture is still an important part of the islands' economy. Sugar cane and pineapples are grown on plantations owned by big companies. Hawaii is the only state that grows coffee, an important crop for Hawaii. Macadamia nuts and papayas are valuable crops, too. Fishing, especially for tuna, is still another source of income, and so are cattle and dairy products. Hawaii's Parker Ranch is the largest cattle ranch on one piece of land in the United States.

Times Telephone Numbers:
MAdison 9-4411—Classified Advertising.
MAdison 5-2345—For all other calls.
Circulation—Largest in the West:
484,000 Daily; 878,000 Sunday.

Los Angeles T

EQUAL RIGHTS

LIBERTY UNDER THE LAW

TRUE INDUSTRIA

VOL. LXXVIII   IN FOUR PARTS   CC ★

FRIDAY MORNING, MARCH 13, 1959

HAWAII WINS APPROVAL A

Macmillan Stills Fears of Adenauer

Agrees to Parley on Central Europe Troop Limitation

BONN, March 12 (UPI)
British Prime Minister Macmillan told Chancellor Adenauer here today that Brit-

More than seven million people visit Hawaii every year.

No industry puts more money in Hawaiians' pockets than the tourist industry. The second largest source of income is the United States military, which pumps more than $4 billion a year into the economy. Despite its big role in Hawaii's economy, agriculture comes in third.

Many people are working to keep the native culture alive. The Hawaiian language is dying out. In 1990 only 8,872 people spoke it, and few children were learning it. Today many people are trying to revive the language by teaching it at school and speaking it at home. Among young Hawaiians, there is a new interest in exploring family roots and the histories of the islands before Captain Cook arrived.

imes

PART I

ALL THE NEWS
ALL THE TIME

84 PAGES

DAILY 10¢

50TH STATE

House Vote Sends Bill to Eisenhower; Signature Pledged

BY ROBERT T. HARTMANN
Times Washington Bureau Chief
WASHINGTON, March 12—Only President Eisenhower's pledged signature stood between Hawaii and its 40-year dream of statehood as Congr...

Hawaii was the last state to be admitted into the Union.

Every now and then, some Hawaiians call for a return to the time when kings and queens ruled Hawaii. The days of King Kamehameha and Queen Liliuokalani are long gone, but the culture Hawaii's monarchy represented still shapes daily life in Hawaii in many ways. The native Hawaiian traditions will always be remembered.

To Hawaiians, performing the hula dance is a way to show pride in their culture.